Close-up Continents

Mapping Africa

Paul Rockett

★

with artwork by Mark Ruffle

W
FRANKLIN WATTS
LONDON • SYDNEY

Franklin Watts
First published in Great Britain in 2015 by
The Watts Publishing Group

Copyright © The Watts Publishing Group 2015

All rights reserved

Editor: Adrian Cole
Series design and illustration: Mark Ruffle
www.rufflebrothers.com

Franklin Watts
An imprint of Hachette Children's Group
Part of The Watts Publishing Group
Carmelite House
50 Victoria Embankment
London EC4Y 0DZ

An Hachette UK Company.
www.hachette.co.uk

www.franklinwatts.co.uk

Picture credits:
Catalan Atlas 1375, detail: 9tr; Ulrich Doering/
Alamy: 16t; Great Stock PL/Alamy: 22b; Justin
Hall, Culver City/Wikimedia Commons: 14bl;
Bruno de Hogues/Gettyimages: 27c; l'Illustra-
tion/Wikimedia Commons: 10cr; imageBroker/
Alamy: 13br; Anton Ivanov/Shutterstock: 19t;
jelldragon/Alamy: 13cr; Eric Laffourgue/Alamy:
24t; Marka/Alamy: 18b; Wayne Parsons/Getty
Images: 20b; Photosky/Dreamstime: 17b; Pho-
togenes: 27t; Patrick Poendi/Dreamstime: 12tr;
Princeton University: 4b; Temps/Shutterstock:
17t; Tommy Trenchard/Alamy: 22c; Watchthe-
world/Shutterstock: 18t; Wikimedia Commons:
flags; Worldshots/Dreamstime: 23b.

Dewey number: 916
HB ISBN: 978 1 4451 4111 4

Printed in China

MIX
Paper from
responsible sources
FSC® C104740
FSC
www.fsc.org

Contents

Where is Africa?

Africa is the second largest continent in the world and covers over one-fifth of the Earth's surface. Its mainland is connected to Asia by a narrow stretch of land, while large oceans and sea surround the rest of the continent.

The border between Egypt and Israel is also the border between Africa and the continent of Asia.

Mediterranean Sea

Israel

Egypt

Asia

Atlantic Ocean

Indian Ocean

Mainland

The mainland of Africa is so large that you can fit the USA, China, India, Argentina and Western Europe in it, and still have extra land to spare.

USA

India

Argentina

Western Europe

China

Africa:
30,301,596 sq km
Other named areas:
29,843,826 sq km

Madagascar

The continent of Africa includes six islands that surround the mainland; Madagascar is the largest.

Early map

One of the earliest maps of Africa was made by the German mapmaker Sebastian Münster, in around 1544. It was made from information gathered by European explorers, and much of it was incorrect.

The Equator

The Equator is an imaginary line running around the widest part of the Earth, halfway between the North Pole and the South Pole. It divides the Earth into the Northern Hemisphere and the Southern Hemisphere.

The Equator runs through the African countries of Gabon, Republic of Congo, Democratic Republic of Congo, Uganda, Kenya and Somalia.

The Tropics

The Tropics are imaginary lines that run around the Earth where temperatures are high all-year round.

The Tropic of Cancer runs around the Earth about 23.5 degrees north of the Equator and goes through the African countries of Algeria, Niger, Libya, Egypt, Mali, Mauritania, Chad and Morocco.

The Tropic of Capricorn runs about 23.5 degrees south of the Equator and goes through the African countries of Namibia, Botswana, South Africa, Mozambique and Madagascar.

Locating Africa

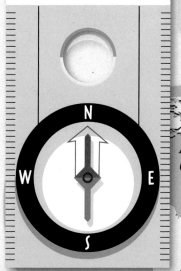

We can describe the location of Africa in relation to the areas of land and water that surround it as well as using the points on a compass.

- Africa is west of Asia

- Africa is south of Europe

- Africa is between the Atlantic Ocean and the Indian Ocean

5

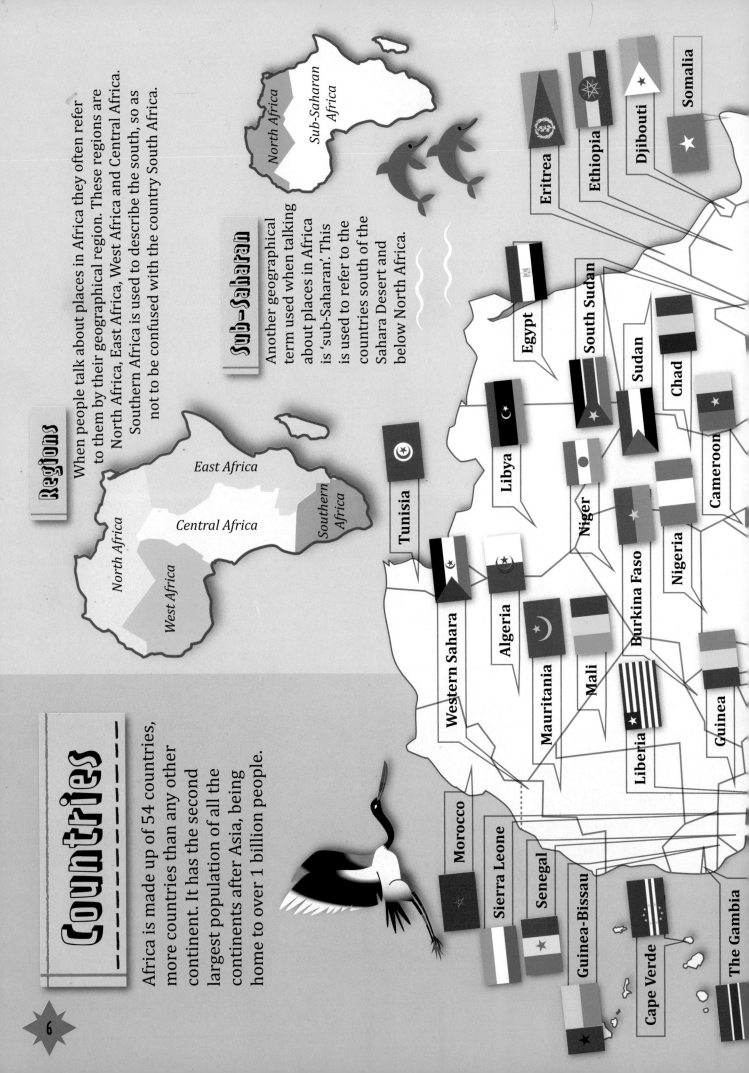

Countries

Africa is made up of 54 countries, more countries than any other continent. It has the second largest population of all the continents after Asia, being home to over 1 billion people.

Regions

When people talk about places in Africa they often refer to them by their geographical region. These regions are North Africa, East Africa, West Africa and Central Africa. Southern Africa is used to describe the south, so as not to be confused with the country South Africa.

North Africa

East Africa

Central Africa

West Africa

Southern Africa

Sub-Saharan

Another geographical term used when talking about places in Africa is 'sub-Saharan'. This is used to refer to the countries south of the Sahara Desert and below North Africa.

North Africa

Sub-Saharan Africa

Tunisia

Morocco

Western Sahara

Algeria

Mauritania

Mali

Senegal

Sierra Leone

Guinea-Bissau

Cape Verde

The Gambia

Liberia

Guinea

Libya

Egypt

Niger

Burkina Faso

Nigeria

Cameroon

South Sudan

Sudan

Chad

Eritrea

Ethiopia

Djibouti

Somalia

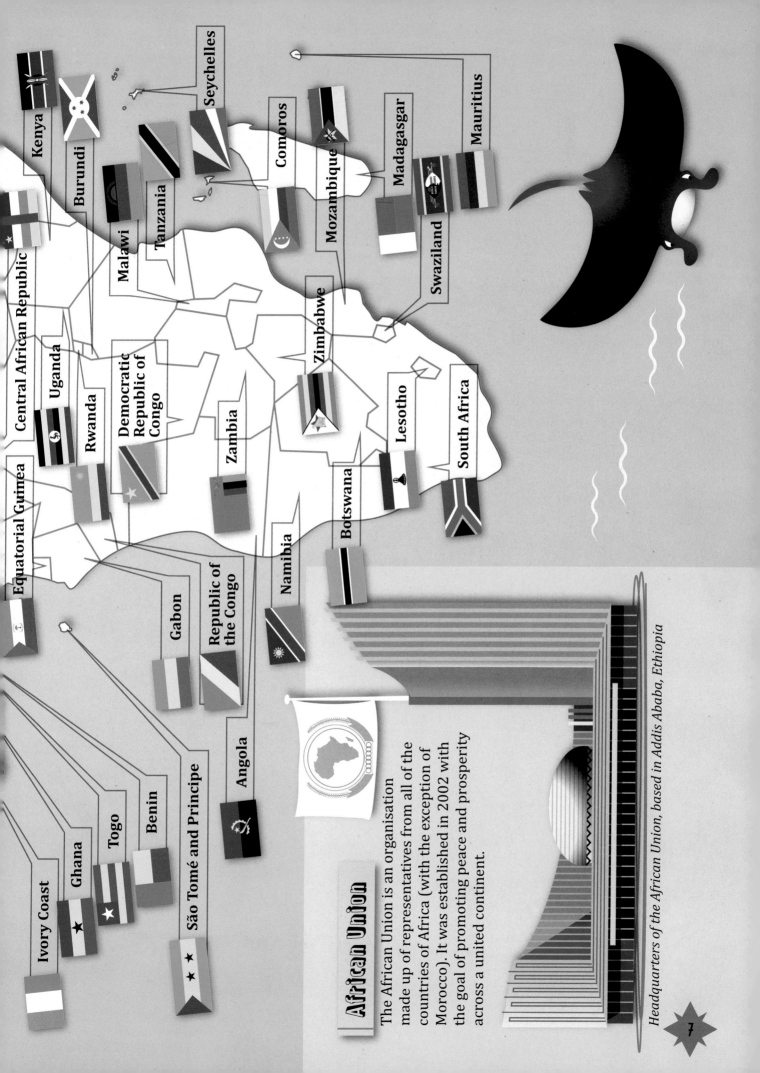

Kenya

Burundi

Central African Republic

Seychelles

Comoros

Madagasgar

Mauritius

Mozambique

Malawi

Tanzania

Uganda

Swaziland

Rwanda

Democratic Republic of Congo

Zimbabwe

Zambia

Equatorial Guinea

Lesotho

South Africa

Botswana

Gabon

Republic of the Congo

Namibia

Angola

São Tomé and Principe

Benin

Togo

Ghana

Ivory Coast

African Union

The African Union is an organisation made up of representatives from all of the countries of Africa (with the exception of Morocco). It was established in 2002 with the goal of promoting peace and prosperity across a united continent.

Headquarters of the African Union, based in Addis Ababa, Ethiopia

Early migration and empires

For many, Africa is seen as the root from which all human life has grown. The oldest human bones have been discovered here. It's also home to some of the wealthiest and oldest empires and civilisations in the world.

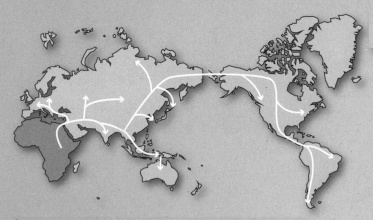

The cradle of humanity

Africa is sometimes referred to as the 'cradle of humanity' because many experts believe that all human ancestors evolved here. Over thousands of years, descendants of these people travelled to live in other parts of the world.

Early kingdoms and empires

Africa has seen the rise and fall of great kingdoms and empires. Kings and leaders controlled entire regions, building fortunes, trade links and developing crafts.

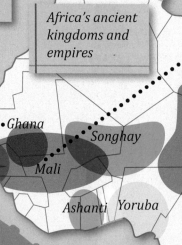

Africa's ancient kingdoms and empires

Carthage

Ancient Egypt

Ghana

Songhay

Wolof

Mali

Kanem-Bornu

Kush

Axum

Ethiopia

Ashanti

Yoruba

Buganda

Rwanda

Luba

Congo

Lunda

Malawi

Lozi

Kilwa

Monomotapa

Merina

Zulu Kingdom

Empire of Ghana
(c. 700 CE–1235)

The Empire of Ghana was formed when tribes united under the first king, Dinga Cisse. It became wealthy through gold mining and the use of camels to transport goods across the Sahara Desert. This was an important development in the history of Africa, as it opened up trade links with other nations.

What happened?
By the 11th century the Empire's power had weakened as competition for trade improved in other parts of Africa. Finally, it came under attack from neighbouring empires, becoming part of the Mali Empire.

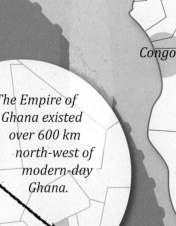

The Empire of Ghana existed over 600 km north-west of modern-day Ghana.

Ghana

Modern-day Ghana

Mali Empire (1230–1600)

A strong leader, called Sundiata Keita, united the region of the Mali Empire. It covered the area of ancient Ghana as well as parts of modern-day Mali, Niger and Guinea.

The Empire became wealthy through trade in gold, salt and slaves. One of the most famous rulers Mansa Musa (c. 1280–1337) is thought by some historians to have been the wealthiest person in history.

What happened?
The Empire eventually lost power through weak rulers and raids from neighbouring countries.

Sundiata Keita

Fourteenth century portrait of wealthy ruler Mansa Musa holding up a gold nugget.

Ancient Egypt (c. 3000 BCE–30 BCE)

Ancient Egypt grew out of small tribal settlements formed along the River Nile, an important source of water for growing crops. The tribes gradually unified and were governed by a pharaoh – a ruler that was thought to be both a man and a god. There were over 170 pharaohs that ruled during the period of ancient Egypt.

What happened?
The ancient civilisation eventually fell under the rule of European empires, first the Greek and then the Roman Empire.

The ancient Egyptians invented lots of things we still use today:

Paper

Pens

Keys

Locks

Toothpaste

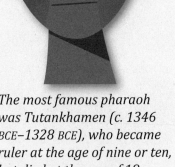

The most famous pharaoh was Tutankhamen (c. 1346 BCE–1328 BCE), who became ruler at the age of nine or ten, but died at the age of 18.

Slave trade

In the 7th century, traders from Arabia, in western Asia, were shipping slaves from Africa to India, Turkey and Persia. In the 15th century sailors from Europe arrived and the slave trade grew. European countries had colonies in the Americas and shipped African slaves there to be sold as labour. As a result there are many descendants of Africans living in the Americas. The terms African-American, African-Caribbean and African-Brazilian are often used to connect them to their roots in Africa.

Mapping independence

From the 15th century, the countries and borders of Africa began facing major changes, and were reshaped by European rulers. It's only in recent history that Africans have been able to take back control of their lands and map out their own futures.

Scramble for Africa

Europe had begun establishing small colonies in Africa in the 15th century. But by the second half of the 19th century there was a rush to grab vast areas of land – this is known as the 'scramble for Africa'.

To avoid conflict over who could take which land, a meeting was held in which the European powers divided up the continent. This was the Berlin Conference (1884–1885). Land was carved up with a focus on trade and resources that suited Europe; the people of Africa had no say on the borders drawn over their homelands.

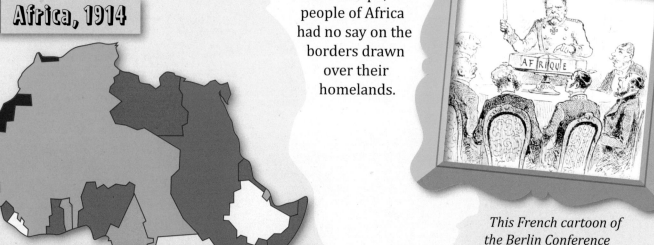

This French cartoon of the Berlin Conference shows the German ruler dividing Africa like a cake. It's titled 'Everyone gets his share'.

Africa, 1914

By 1914, European countries had claimed nearly 90 per cent of African territory.

France

Great Britain

Belgium

Spain

Italy

Germany

Portugal

Independent

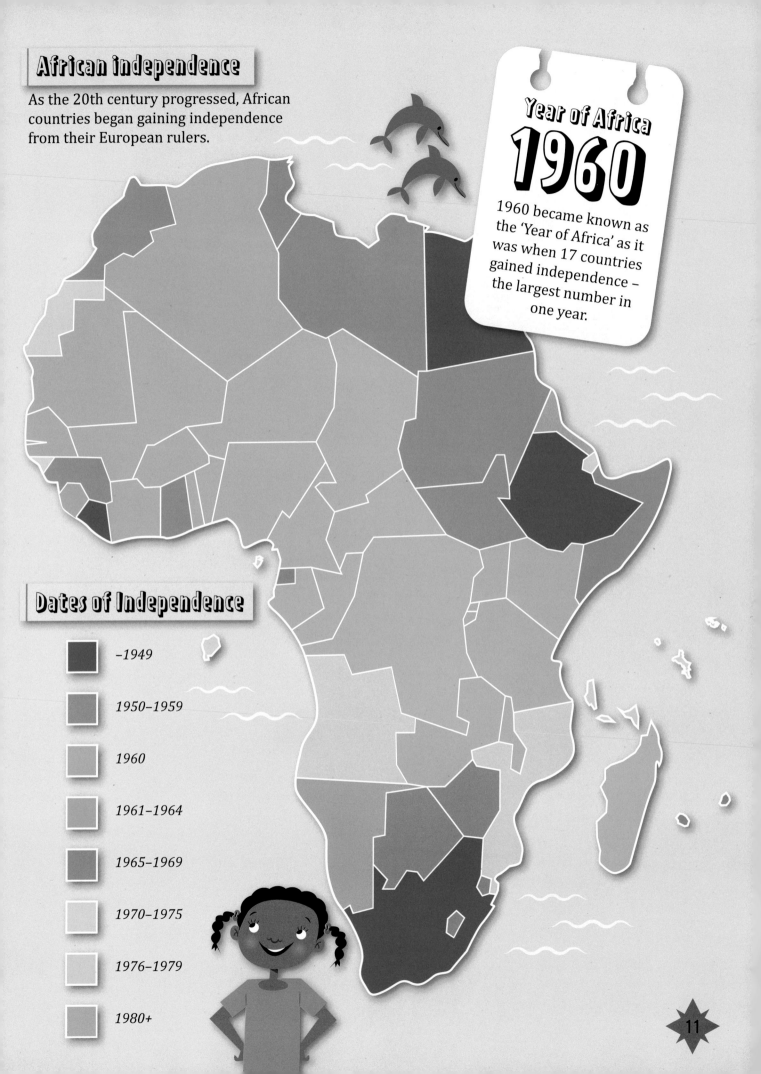

African independence

As the 20th century progressed, African countries began gaining independence from their European rulers.

Year of Africa
1960

1960 became known as the 'Year of Africa' as it was when 17 countries gained independence – the largest number in one year.

Dates of Independence

- –1949
- 1950–1959
- 1960
- 1961–1964
- 1965–1969
- 1970–1975
- 1976–1979
- 1980+

Climates

Africa is the hottest continent in the world. It has five climate zones but two cover most of the continent. These zones create Africa's vast area of tropical rainforest and dry deserts.

50°C

0°C

Sahara Desert

Climate zones:

- [ ] dry
- tropical humid
- humid subtropical
- marine west coast
- Mediterranean

Tropic of Cancer

Tropical rainforests

The tropical regions either side of the Equator receive high levels of sunlight and rainfall. These provide the perfect conditions for plant growth, creating areas of dense rainforest.

Water falls from clouds as rain

Equator

Heat from the Sun causes water to evaporate, rising into the air, forming clouds as it cools

Tropic of Capricorn

Namib Desert

Kalahari Desert

Cooler climates

The coastal regions in the north and south of Africa experience weather that is more varied. This is because they are exposed to areas of the ocean that bring along different temperatures through the movement of ocean currents and wind.

Deserts

The areas further north and south of the Tropics experience short, dry winters and less rainfall. In the areas where rainfall is very scarce there are deserts. To the north is the Sahara Desert, and to the south is the Kalahari and Namib Desert.

Sahara Desert

The Sahara Desert covers most of North Africa and is the world's hottest desert. During cloudless hot summer days the temperature can go beyond 50^0C. However, at night the heat from the day rises and the temperature drops sharply to below 0^0C.

Droughts

Droughts occur when an area receives no rain over a long period of time. Without rain, crops cannot grow and the soil dries up.

In 2011, the east African countries, Somalia, Ethiopia and Kenya, experienced their lowest rainfall levels in 60 years. This led to a long drought that affected millions of people. Harvests failed and food prices rose. People went hungry and many died from starvation.

Highland climate

High mountainous areas are known as 'highlands'. The climate here is different to the climate found in the surrounding lowlands. This is because the temperature reduces, the higher the altitude.

To combat droughts, many local and international charities have been building wells to underground water sources and constructing irrigation systems that keep crops watered.

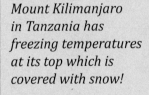

Mount Kilimanjaro in Tanzania has freezing temperatures at its top which is covered with snow!

The Eastern Highlands in Zimbabwe have a much cooler and wetter climate to that of the surrounding lowland.

Eastern Highlands average altitude: 1,200–1,600 m.

Eastern Lowlands average altitude: 600–900 m.

Wildlife

From deserts to rainforests, and savannas in between, Africa has a vast natural landscape that houses some of the world's most endangered and deadly creatures.

African savanna

Savannas are stretches of grassland. The abundance of tall grass and open plains attracts grazing animals such as zebras, gazelles and giraffes. These animals attract their predators: lions, cheetahs and leopards.

Lion

Giraffe

Grass

Zebra

Savanna

Black mamba

Okavango Delta

Within the arid landscape and open savanna of Botswana is a large, wet area of land, called the Okavango Delta. Most deltas are formed where rivers meet the sea, but the Okavango Delta is created by water from the Okavango river emptying out onto the land.

Elephant

Okavango river

Lemur

Hippopotamus

The Okavango Delta's combination of both dry and wetland attracts a wealth of wildlife, such as rhinoceros, hippopotamus, lechwe and warthog.

14

Critically endangered!

Africa is home to some of the world's most endangered animals. Many are hunted for sport, trophies or medicines. The effects of deforestation have left many species homeless and unable to survive outside of their natural habitats.

African wild ass estimated population: 200

Cross River gorilla estimated population: 300

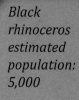

Tiny terrors

Although Africa is home to large, fierce predators, such as lions and crocodiles, some of its most dangerous creatures are tiny and hard to spot.

Black rhinoceros estimated population: 5,000

Tsetse flies live by feeding off the blood of animals.

The female mosquito bites into mammals to get blood which helps fertilise her eggs.

Tsetse fly

A tsetse fly bite can transmit a disease known as sleeping sickness. This causes a fever and impacts on the nervous system. It can be fatal if not treated.

Guinea-worm

Guinea-worms are disease-spreading parasites that grow inside humans. The worms wriggle out through the person's skin, often through the legs and feet. Although not deadly, guinea-worm disease can make it difficult for the carrier to walk.

Baobabs

There are eight species of baobab tree, six of which can be found in Madagascar. They have huge swollen trunks that store large amounts of water, helping them to survive through periods of drought.

Mosquito

Mosquitos spread a number of deadly viruses and diseases, such as yellow fever and malaria. They breed rapidly in warm and wet climates, and are extremely common in Central Africa.

15

Natural landmarks

Across Africa's vast areas of desert and dense forest are giant valleys and mountains that range from the stumpy to the gigantic. It's also home to great lakes, breath-taking waterfalls, as well as a meteorite from outer-space.

Great Rift Valley

The Great Rift Valley runs from the Middle East in Asia through to south-east Africa. Its most dramatic area of landscape is in East Africa and is known as the East African Rift. It's a natural feature that can be seen from space.

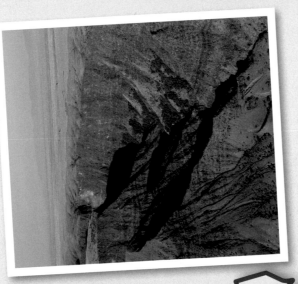

Rift valleys form when the surface of the Earth, its tectonic plates, split apart, creating a deep trench with steep sides. The formation of the Great Rift Valley is ongoing. In a few million years, the weakening surface in the valley may cause the land in eastern Africa to split off into a separate landmass.

River Nile

The River Nile is the longest river in the world. It measures around 6,650 km in length.

Atlas Mountains

The Atlas Mountains stretch across Morocco, Algeria and Tunisia for about 2,000 km. The mountains act as a barrier, preventing moisture blown in from the Mediterranean Sea and the Atlantic Ocean from reaching the desert region.

The African Great Lakes

Contained within the Rift Valley are tall rugged mountains and deep lakes. The African Great Lakes are part of this landscape. They are:

A – Albert **K** – Kivu **M** – Malawi
V – Victoria
Y – Kyoga **T** – Tanganyika
E – Edward

River Nile

Nile Delta

Mediterranean Sea

Tunisia

Morocco

Atlas Mountains

Algeria

Sahara Desert

Niger River

Atlantic Ocean

--- = Rift Valley

East African Rift

Mount Kilimanjaro

Mount Kilimanjaro is a dormant volcano that forms part of the Great Rift Valley. It's also the highest mountain in Africa, at 5,895 m.

Mosi-oa-Tunya (Victoria Falls)

On the border between Zambia and Zimbabwe is the mighty waterfall, Victoria Falls. When Scottish explorer, Dr David Livingstone, stumbled across it in 1855, he was so impressed he named it after Queen Victoria, queen of England at the time.

Zambezi River

Congo River

Kalahari Desert

Namibia

Namib Desert

Fish River Canyon

Fish River Canyon is the largest canyon in Africa. It's 550 m deep, 27 km wide and 160 km long. The slopes of the canyon reveal 1.5 billion years of colourful rock formations.

Inselbergs

Dotted around parts of Africa are knobbly inselbergs – small island mountains. They stand alone on flat plains, and are made of tightly packed rock that is millions of years old.

An inselberg in Nigeria, Wase Rock, measuring 350 m in height

Hoba meteorite

The largest meteorite to have landed on Earth in one piece is in Namibia. It fell to Earth around 80 million years ago, and weighs around 60 tonnes.

Manmade landmarks

Africa's history of ancient civilisations and colonial occupation can be spotted in the impressive buildings and monuments across the continent.

Makam Echahid, Algeria

The Great Mosque of Djenné

The Great Mosque of Djenné is the largest mud brick building in the world. The mud-brick walls are coated in a smooth plaster with sticks poking out.

The first Great Mosque of Djenné was built in the 13th century. The current building dates from 1907 and takes pride of place in the town of Djenné, central Mali.

Independence Arch, Ghana

Basilica of Our Lady of Peace, Ivory Coast

The Great Enclosure

Within the country of Zimbabwe is an area known as Great Zimbabwe, once a grand royal city from the 11th–15th century. Today stands its remains and a striking structure called the Great Enclosure. Its walls are as high as 11 m, and curve 250 m in length.

Churches of Lalibela

Lalibela is a town in the north of Ethiopia that has 11 churches, dating from 12th–13th centuries. These churches have all been carved out of solid rock.

The Church of St George, from Lalibela, is carved in the shape of a cross.

Egypt

Egypt

The country of Egypt is dotted with monuments to the civilisations of its ancient history (see page 9).

Sphinx

Pyramid of Djoser ▲

Pyramid of Sahure ▲

Saqqara ▲▲

Pyramid of Khufu

Pyramids at Dahshur ▲

River Nile

Luxor Temple

Parliament Building, Tanzania

Pyramids

Most pyramids were built as tombs for the rulers of Egypt and their families. To date, over 130 pyramids have been discovered in Egypt.

The largest pyramid is the Pyramid of Khufu, also known as the Great Pyramid of Giza. When this pyramid was finished, in around 2560 BCE, it was 146.5 m tall. It was the tallest manmade structure in the world for over 3,800 years.

Valley of the Kings

Karnak

Abu Simbel

19

Settlements

The settlements in Africa range from the traditional, tribal and nomadic, to past centres of colonialism and modern urban sprawls.

Population density

This map shows the areas of population over Africa. Person per 2.5 square kilometres:

0	1–24	25–129	130–259	260–519	Over 520

Dakar

Dakar is the capital city of Senegal. It is the most westerly point in Africa and sits on a peninsula – a point of land sticking out into the ocean. This makes it the perfect contact point for ships sailing along the Atlantic. Today, it is one of Africa's busiest ports.

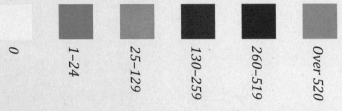

Lagos

Lagos is Nigeria's most populated city, and is the second biggest city in Africa (after Cairo in Egypt).

—— = main highway

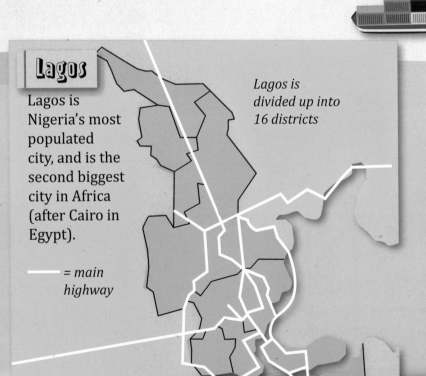

Lagos is divided up into 16 districts

Lagos is one of the fastest growing urban areas in the world, with modern skyscrapers dotting the skyline. Although the city has a big network of roads, they struggle to support the growing population and rising number of car owners.

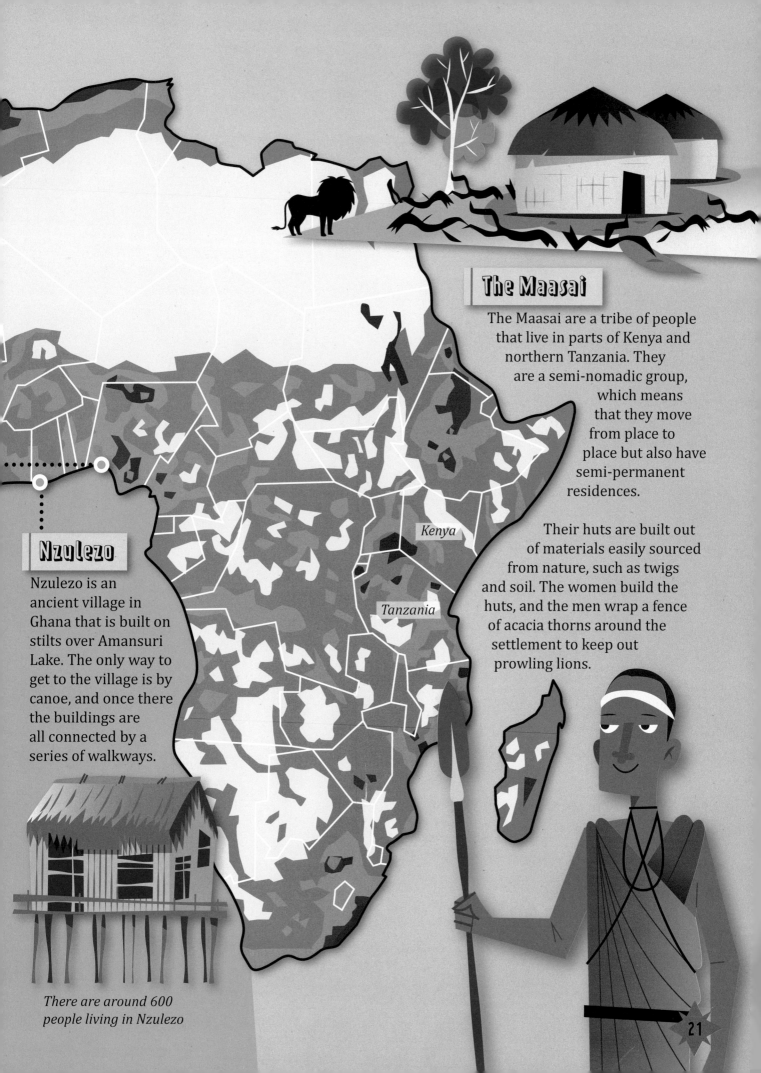

The Maasai

The Maasai are a tribe of people that live in parts of Kenya and northern Tanzania. They are a semi-nomadic group, which means that they move from place to place but also have semi-permanent residences.

Their huts are built out of materials easily sourced from nature, such as twigs and soil. The women build the huts, and the men wrap a fence of acacia thorns around the settlement to keep out prowling lions.

Kenya

Tanzania

Nzulezo

Nzulezo is an ancient village in Ghana that is built on stilts over Amansuri Lake. The only way to get to the village is by canoe, and once there the buildings are all connected by a series of walkways.

There are around 600 people living in Nzulezo

Industry

The giant landmass of Africa contains industries above and below the ground. These include the farming of land for food and cotton, while deep underground the continent is mined for precious metals and minerals.

Main industries in Africa

Crops:
- Sugar
- Corn
- Barley
- Oats
- Tobacco
- Tea
- Coffee
- Rice
- Cotton
- Fruit

Industry:
- Electronics
- Mining
- Textiles
- Timber
- Fishing

Livestock:
- Cattle
- Sheep
- Goats

Sierra Leone

Ghana

Mining

Africa has one of the largest mineral industries in the world. There are underground mines all around the continent, with people extracting precious stones and metals such as rubies and diamonds, gold and uranium.

Diamonds

Sierra Leone is one of the world's largest suppliers of diamonds. This resource should make it one of the richest countries in the world, however it is one of the poorest. The country is still recovering from a brutal civil war (1991–2002), which saw a struggle for the control of diamond mines.

Gold

South Africa is the richest nation in Africa. Its mining of natural resources has been important to its economic success. It is most famous for gold mining. The country has almost 50 per cent of the world's 'found' gold reserves. It also has large coal, platinum and diamond mining industries.

Farming

Farming is the most important industry in Africa. The crops that are grown vary depending on the climate of the region. In the tropical areas, in countries such as Uganda and Cameroon, bananas, yams, tea and coffee are grown.

Bananas

Tea

Yam

Coffee

Wheat

Millet

Barley

In the drier regions, in countries such as Chad and Sudan, cereal crops like wheat and barley are grown.

Chad

Sudan

Cameroon

Uganda

Kenya

Cotton and textiles

Small scale farmers grow the most cotton plants, especially in the savanna areas of Africa.

The production of textiles has always been a core industry in Africa, creating jobs that range from growing cotton to weaving cloth.

Madagascar

South Africa

Kente cloth from Ghana

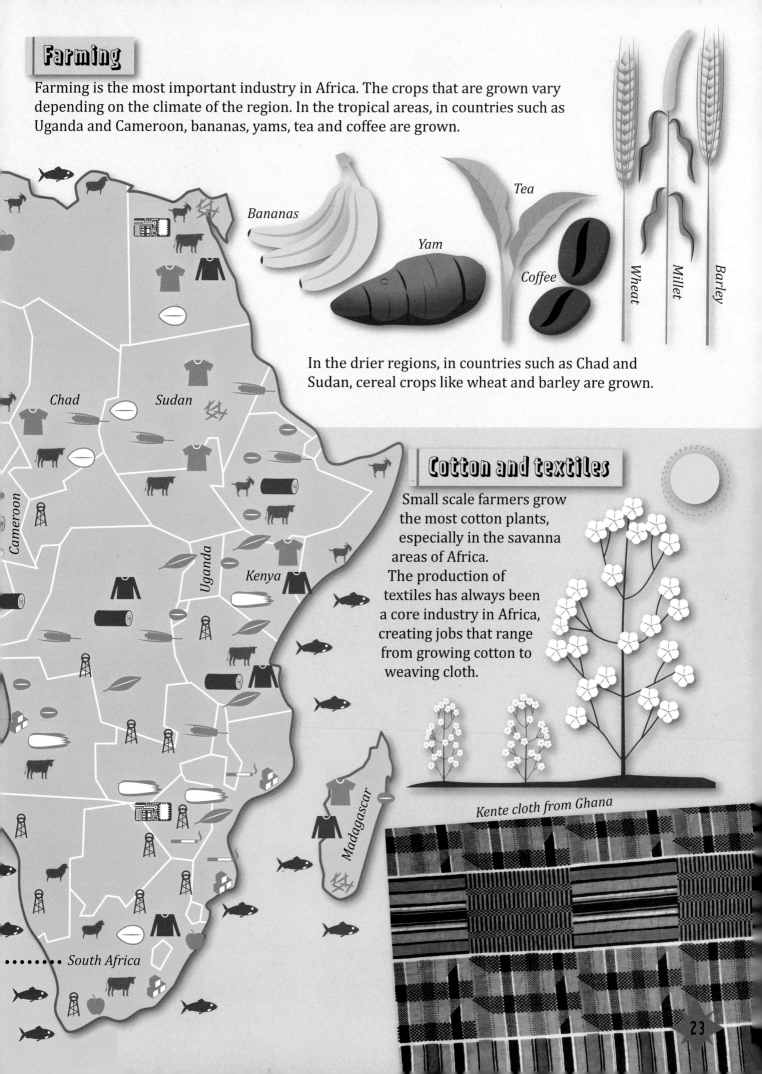

Sport

Sports have been played in Africa since ancient times. Today, African nations continue to produce top international sports stars in athletics, football and rugby.

Mancala

For many people mancala is Africa's national game. It's a board game played in most African countries, though its name may differ. Mancala is Arabic and means 'to transfer' – and this is exactly what you do in the game – you move playing pieces from one cup-shaped dent to another.

Senet

Pieces of a board game called senet have been found buried in ancient Egyptian tombs dating back to 3500 BCE. Senet is played on a grid of 30 squares arranged in three rows of ten. Each player uses a set of pawns, but no one is really sure of the rules.

Nuba wrestling

Wrestling was a popular sport in ancient Egypt and in the area of Nubia, a region along the River Nile that crosses over modern-day Egypt and north Sudan. In Sudan, wrestling, known as Nuba wrestling, is still practised today by many tribes and sportsmen.

Africa Cup of Nations

Football is the most popular sport in Africa. Top players from African nations perform in club games around the world. Africa's own football tournament, the Africa Cup of Nations, is held every two years.

Egypt

Sudan

Ethiopia

Kenya

Rift Valley

24

Long distance running

Both Kenya and Ethiopia have impressive records in producing top long distance runners. One reason why runners from these countries are thought to be so good is because they train in high altitude regions of the Rift Valley.

The low oxygen levels at high altitudes would cause most runners to struggle. However, long-term training here helps the body to adapt, increasing the runner's performance.

Kenenisa Bekele

Born: 13 June 1982

One of the world's top runners, Kenenisa Bekele, is from a village near Bekoji in Ethiopia. As well as having a large collection of medals, he also holds world records in the 5,000 metres (12 minutes 37.35 seconds) and 10,000 metres (26 minutes 17.53 seconds).

Angola

South America

Brazil

Capoeira

Capoeira is a martial art that was developed in the 17th century by West African slaves in Brazil. It combines elements of traditional Angolan dance and acrobatics. While its popularity grew as a form of self-defence, it is now also practised and performed around the world as a sport and a dance.

Culture

The crafts of Africa's past continue to impress and inspire the world. You can see their influences in home decorations, art movements, dance and pop music.

Zellige mosaics

A distinctive feature of many Moroccan buildings is the tiles that cover their walls. The zellige tile is handcrafted from glazed and fired clay, cut into small pieces to form a large mosaic. The mosaics follow geometric patterns that can be simple tessellated shapes or resemble complex mathematical puzzles.

Morocco

Kpanlogo dance

Kwassa kwassa dance

Burkina Faso

Benin

Nigeria

Gabon

Masks

African masks have inspired European art movements, such as Cubism, and are hugely popular tourist souvenirs. Their origins can be traced back to the Stone Age. Masks are different for each tribe.

Mask design worn by Bobo people from Burkina Faso

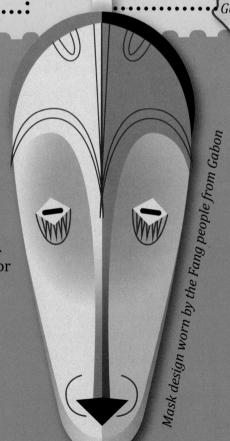

Mask design worn by the Fang people from Gabon

Benin bronzes

The Benin Empire controlled much of modern-day Nigeria between the 15th and 19th centuries. Inside the Benin royal palace there were hundreds of plaques, known as the Benin bronzes, decorating its walls. These plaques show the great skill of metalworkers and artists from the area. The bronzes portray people and events, such as important battles.

Although they are called bronzes, most of the Benin bronzes were made from brass.

Karyenda drum

The karyenda drum is a sacred instrument from Burundi, representing regeneration. It's made from hollowed tree trunks covered with animal skins. The drum is beaten to signal rites and rituals, such as royal coronations, weddings and funerals.

Large groups of drummers, such as the Royal Drummers of Burundi, produce a deep thunderous noise that has proved popular as music in its own right.

Burundi

Religion

Much of Africa's traditional folk art, dance and music have a connection with a tribal religion. While some of these ancient beliefs have survived, the vast majority of Africa is dominated by Islamic and Christian faiths. These religions roughly split the continent in two: Islam in the north and east, Christianity in the south.

Indlamu, Zulu dance

Islam ☐   Christianity ☐

27

Food and drink

Food in Africa features a large variety of meats and spices. Most food comes from local sources of crops and cattle, with the odd wild animal for extra bite.

Spices

Spices play an important part in Moroccan food. They are sold at markets, known as souks, piled high in large sacks and tubs. Bright colourful spices, such as cumin, paprika and saffron, are used to flavour stews as well as desserts.

Tsebhi

Tsebhi is a traditional Eritrean stew made with beef or lamb. Its spicy, bitter-sweet flavour comes from a herb mixture that includes ginger, cloves, fenugreek seeds and chillies.

Cassava

Nigeria is the world's largest producer of cassava, one of the most important foods in Africa. The plant grows well in humid climates and can also survive dry, drought-affected soil better than most crops. It's grown for its fat roots, which are often dried and ground into flour. It is used to make bread and dishes such as tapioca.

The cassava plant is not a native African plant. It comes from South America and was introduced to Africa by Portuguese traders in the 16th century.

Tagine pot, used for cooking stews, also called tagines

Himbasha bread

Ugali, a thick porridge-like dish made from cornflour

Fufu

Fufu is an African dish popular in Ghana. It's a sticky dough-like ball that is served with soups. It's made by boiling yams, plantains or cassava until soft and then pounding them into a paste.

Gonimbrasia belina moth (edible caterpillars)

Biltong

Biltong is a traditional South African snack of strips of dried, cured meat. Biltong is usually made from beef, but is can also be made from the meat of impala, wildebeest and ostrich.

Braai

On 24 September, South Africans celebrate National Heritage Day. On this day the country recognises its culture and history. Many people celebrate by having a 'braai' – Afrikaans for barbecue. A braai is considered an important part of South Africa's culture. In fact many people now refer to National Heritage Day as National Braai Day.

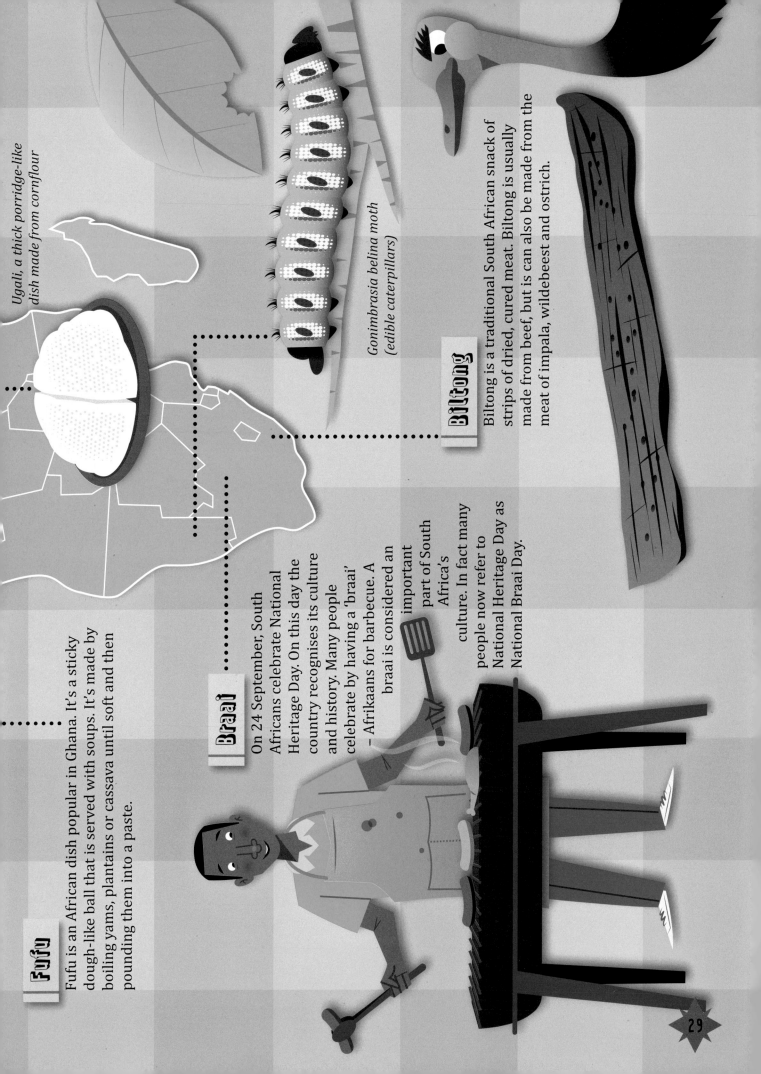

COUNTRY	SIZE SQ KM	POPULATION	CAPITAL CITY	MAIN LANGUAGES*
Nigeria	923,768	181,562,056	Abuja	English
Ethiopia	1,104,300	99,465,819	Addis Ababa	Amharic, Oromo, Somali, Trigrigna
Egypt	1,001,450	88,487,396	Cairo	Arabic
Democratic Republic of Congo	2,344,858	79,375,136	Kinshasa	French
South Africa	1,219,090	53,675,563	Pretoria, Cape Town, Bloemfontein	Afrikaans, Northern Sotho, English, Southern Ndebele, Swazi, Xhosa, Zulu
Tanzania	947,300	51,045,882	Dodoma	Swahili, English
Kenya	580,367	45,925,301	Nairobi	English, Kiswahili
Algeria	2,381,741	39,542,166	Algiers	Arabic
Uganda	241,038	37,101,745	Kampala	English
Sudan	1,861,484	36,108,853	Khartoum	Arabic, English
Morocco	446,550	33,322,699	Rabat	Arabic, Berber
Ghana	238,533	26,327,649	Accra	English
Mozambique	799,380	25,303,113	Maputo	Portuguese, Makhuwa
Madagascar	587,041	23,812,681	Antananarivo	Malagasy, French
Cameroon	475,440	23,739,218	Yaoundé	French, English
Ivory Coast	322,463	23,295,302	Yamoussoukro	French
Angola	1,246,700	19,625,353	Luanda	Portuguese
Burkina Faso	274,200	18,931,686	Ouagadougou	French
Niger	1,267,000	18,045,729	Niamey	French
Malawi	118,484	17,964,697	Lilongwe	Chichewa, English
Mali	1,240,192	16,955,536	Bamako	French, Bambara
Zambia	752,618	15,066,266	Lusaka	English, many Batu languages
Zimbabwe	390,757	14,229,541	Harare	Shona, Ndebele, English, Tonga, Tswana, Chewa
Senegal	196,722	13,975,834	Dakar	French
Rwanda	26,338	12,661,733	Kigali	Kinyarwanda, French, English
South Sudan	644,329	12,042,910	Juba	English
Guinea	245,857	11,780,162	Conakry	French
Chad	1,284,000	11,631,456	N'Djamena	French
Tunisia	163,610	11,037,225	Tunis	Arabic
Burundi	27,830	10,742,276	Bujumbura	Kirundi, French
Somalia	637,657	10,616,380	Mogadishu	Somali, Arabic
Benin	112,622	10,448,647	Porto-Novo	French, Yoruba
Togo	56,785	7,552,318	Lomé	French
Eritrea	117,600	6,527,689	Asmara	Tigrinya, Arabic, English
Libya	1,759,540	6,411,776	Tripoli	Arabic
Sierra Leone	71,740	5,879,098	Freetown	English
Central African Republic	622,984	5,391,539	Bangui	Sangho, French
Republic of the Congo	342,000	4,755,097	Brazzaville	French
Liberia	111,369	4,195,666	Monrovia	English
Mauritania	1,030,700	3,596,702	Nouakchott	Arabic
Namibia	824,292	2,212,307	Windhoek	English, Afrikaans
Botswana	581,730	2,182,719	Gaborone	English, Setswana
The Gambia	11,300	1,967,709	Banjul	English
Lesotho	30,355	1,947,701	Maseru	Sesotho, English
Guinea-Bissau	36,125	1,726,170	Bissau	Portuguese
Gabon	267,667	1,705,336	Libreville	French
Swaziland	17,364	1,435,613	Lobamba, Mbabane	Siswati, English
Mauritius	2,040	1,339,827	Port Louis	Creole, English
Djibouti	23,200	828,324	Djibouti City	French, Arabic
Comoros	2,235	780,971	Moroni	Shikomoro, Arabic, French
Equatorial Guinea	28,051	740,743	Malabo	Spanish, French
Western Sahara	266,000	570,866	Laayoune	Arabic
Cape Verde	4,033	545,993	Praia	Portuguese
São Tomé and Principe	964	194,006	São Tomé	Portuguese
Seychelles	455	92,430	Victoria	French, English, Seychellois Creole

* There are thousands of languages that have survived from the tribes of Africa's pre-colonial era. While not listed as being a main language of any country, many are still in use.

Glossary

acacia
a thorny tree that grows in warm countries, with yellow or white flowers

altitude
the height of something measured in relation to a given point, such as sea level

civilisations
communities that are well-organised with advanced social developments, often forming the basis for later nations

climate
average weather conditions in a particular area

colonies
countries or areas controlled by another country and occupied by settlers from that country

currents
bodies of water or air continually moving in the same direction

deforestation
the cutting down and removal of trees in a forested area

delta
a triangular-shaped piece of land that is formed when a river splits into smaller rivers, usually before it flows into an ocean

endangered
at risk of extinction (dying out)

Equator
an imaginary line drawn around the Earth separating the Northern and Southern hemispheres

hemisphere
half of a sphere, such as the sections of the Earth divided by the Equator

heritage
where you have come from, including items of historical importance and traditions from the past

humidity
amount of water vapour in the air

meteorite
the name for a piece of rock from outer-space that has landed on Earth

migration
movement of people and animals from one region to another

prosperity
the state of being successful, especially in terms of making money

rites
a religious act or traditional ceremony that marks a special occasion, such as baptisms and funerals

savanna
a large flat area of land in tropical regions with lots of grass and few trees

souks
largely open-air market places, found in Muslim regions in North Africa and the Middle East

tectonic plates
large, slow-moving sections of the Earth's crust

tessellated
formed by small blocks arranged into a pattern, such as on a mosaic or a chequered board

textiles
material woven or knitted together, such as cloth

Tropics
the two imaginary lines that surround the Equator and the region inside this area, which is the hottest part of the world

Index